know the game

Athletics

by Carl T. Johnson, National Coach (North), BAAB.

CONTENTS

FOREWORD

In a sport so varied and comprehensive that there are no less than thirty-eight separate athletic events in the Olympic programme there would be no difficulty in finding sufficient material for a massive compendium or a series of shorter specialist volumes, so to contain the essential rules and the nub of training and competition advice in one slim booklet is a formidable task. Creditably Carlton Johnson has achieved this in a manner that retains the interest, and serves the interests, of the organiser, the judge, the coach and the athlete.

There is an unfortunate tendency nowadays to think of athletics almost solely in terms of championships and records, ignoring the fact that for the majority of participants in this oldest and most fundamental of sports the pleasure lies in the actual participation, and the reward in the sense of physical and mental satisfaction that comes with even the most modest achievement in one of the many varied skills and activities that comprise athletics.

Every type of physique can be catered for by at least one of the running, jumping, throwing or walking groups of events and just to complete the course, throw or jump any distance at all in the correct manner or to clear a cross-bar provides a measurable achievement, whether it be assessed on a decathlon scoring table or in an award scheme.

There is no sport with a wider base . . . every school-child who is not lame or infirm, runs, jumps and throws . . . and the talented can emerge to progress up the pyramid.

This book, catering as it does for those at the base, worthily provides for the great good of a great number, and I hope that all those who have the good fortune to use it and profit from it will share the pleasure and enjoyment that athletics brings to its devotees all over the world.

Arthur Gold

Honorary Secretary
British Amateur Athletic Board

INTRODUCTION

Running has flourished as a sport since earliest times, even since before the first recorded Olympic Games in 776 BC. The other modern athletic disciplines, however, have developed over many centuries through man's natural instinct to compete against others in throwing or in jumping as far or as high as possible.

Modern Track and Field is an amalgam of many different activities. Those events which did not begin in Greek times have in most part grown from the contests of rural medieval Europe, and reflect their parenthood in their rules. Wall leaping in Cumberland and wheel throwing in Ireland gave rise to Pole Vault and Hammer Throw. Discus Throwing and Javelin Throwing with their metric specifications reflect their continental development.

During the late nineteenth century local interpretations of the rules were modified, firstly in the universities where competitive athletics became organised, and later through the development of the international and Olympic movements, and by 1912 had assumed their present-day form. Few changes have been made since.

The sport however is still developing, with the throwing events beginning to outgrow the confines of the arena, and more events becoming accepted as suitable for women. In recent times we have witnessed the introduction of 400m Hurdles for women, and 1500m and 3000m races also. Women even run in marathons. How long will it be before they are Triple Jumping or Hammer Throwing?

There are in England alone some 500 athletic clubs, and it is as a member of such a club that the aspirations of a developing athlete can best be realised. No good quality athlete has succeeded in making the grade entirely on his own. All athletes need the encouragement, coaching and competitive opportunity afforded by the athletics club. Unless you live in one of the more remote parts of Britain, an athletic club should exist within a few miles of your home. The addresses of such clubs are available through the British Amateur Athletic Board, which is the overall governing body of athletics for both men and women in the United Kingdom.

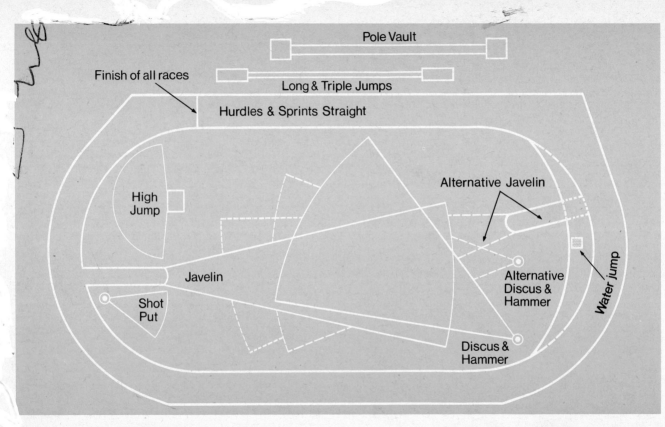

Pole Vault

Finish of all races

Long & Triple Jumps

Hurdles & Sprints Straight

High Jump

Alternative Javelin

Javelin

Alternative Discus & Hammer

Shot Put

Discus & Hammer

Water Jump

The Layout of a standard 400m athletics arena.

TRACK GEOGRAPHY

The modern track is elliptical in shape, having two parallel straights joined by two semi-circular bends, and measuring 400m around at a distance of 30cms out from the inside edge. This basic plan, together with a standard placement of field event facilities on the infield, is accepted with only minor local deviations throughout the world.

Considerations such as the direction of the prevailing wind, and the position of the afternoon sun, are important when determining the initial siting of the track, especially when laying down temporary tracks on school playing fields. Neither of these should be allowed to affect adversely either competitors or spectators. Whilst the detrimental effect of an adverse wind upon runners is obvious, that of the sun upon field event competitors in particular is more obscure.

Sprint races are run in lanes throughout. The 100m is run entirely on a straight track. The 200m takes place around the half-lap of a standard track, commencing on a bend and finishing at the far end of the straight. The 400m takes place around one complete lap of the track. In all races the athletes run so that their left side is nearer to the inside of the track, i.e. around a left-hand bend.

Lanes must be a minimum of 1·22m wide and race distances should be individually measured in each lane at a distance of 20cms from the inside border (with the exception of the first lane, which is measured 30cms from the inside border) so that no runner gains a distance advantage over another. The 200m and 400m races therefore have staggered starts.

Lanes are numbered from inside to outside in consecutive numerical order, or from left to right on a straight track.

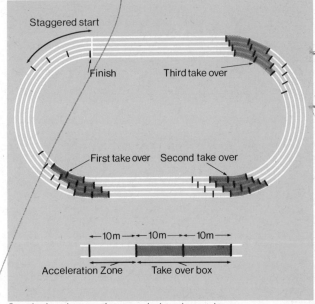

Standard track stepped starts and relay take over boxes.

The Start

The start line, measuring 5cms wide (as do all boundary lines), is drawn across the track at right angles to the inner edge, so that the distance from its *nearer* edge to the *nearer* edge of the finish line is the exact distance of the race.

Races at 200m and 400m have staggered starts and in races over 400m a curved start line should be used. At international level staggered starts are used for 800m races also, and the first 300m of the race is run in lanes.

Finish

A common finish of all races is conventionally situated at the end of the 'home' straight.

It is marked by a line drawn at right angles to the inside edge of the track.

Relay Racing

The 4 x 100m relay requires that the track be marked with 20m long take-over 'boxes', usually in blue paint, in each lane. The box boundaries are situated 10m either side of the scratch lines marked at 100m, 200m, and 300m distance from the finish. Acceleration zones, starting 10m before the nearer boundary line of each box, should be clearly indicated (usually in yellow paint) at all change-over stations.

The take-over box for the 4 x 400m relay is constructed 10m either side of the finish line, and running parallel to it.

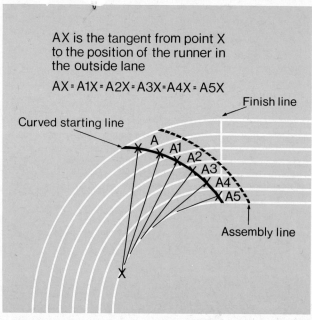

AX is the tangent from point X to the position of the runner in the outside lane

AX = A1X = A2X = A3X = A4X = A5X

Finish line

Curved starting line

A
A1
A2
A3
A4
A5

X

Assembly line

Construction of the Curved Start.

Table of staggered starts on a 84.39 m by 73 m track

	Distance beyond previous scratch line on inside			
	At 100 m Or Third Change	At 200 m Or Second Change	At 300 m Or First Change	At 400 m
Lane 1	Scratch mark	Scratch mark	Scratch mark	Scratch mark
Lane 2	1.799 m	3.518 m	3.518 m	7.037 m
Lane 3	1.916 m	3.833 m	3.833 m	7.666 m
Lane 4	1.916 m	3.833 m	3.833 m	7.666 m
Lane 5	1.916 m	3.833 m	3.833 m	7.666 m
Lane 6	1.916 m	3.833 m	3.833 m	7.666 m

Spacings differ from those given for all tracks not measuring 84.39 m by 73 m.
Staggers are best marked by measuring back from the finish with a 100 m tape.

Table of Hurdle specifications.

Race Distance	Age Group	Height of Barrier	No of Barriers	Approach to first Barrier	Interval between Barriers	Distance last Hurdle to Finish
	MALE					
110 m	Adult	106.7 cm	10	13.72 m	9.14 m	14.02 m
110 m	U19	99.0 cm	10	13.72 m	9.14 m	14.02 m
100 m	U17	91.4 cm	10	13.0 m	8.5 m	10.5 m
80 m	U15	84.5 cm	8	12.0 m	8.0 m	12.0 m
75 m	U14	76.2 cm	8	11.5 m	7.5 m	11.0 m
70 m	U13	68.0 cm	8	11.0 m	7.0 m	10.0 m
	FEMALE					
100 m	Adult	83.8 cm	10	13.0 m	8.5 m	10.5 m
80 m	U17	76.2 cm	8	12.0 m	8.0 m	12.0 m
75 m	U15	76.2 cm	8	11.5 m	7.5 m	11.0 m
70 m	U13	68.0 cm	8	11.0 m	7.0 m	10.0 m
Special Hurdle races						
	MALE					
400 m	Over 17	91.4 cm	10	45.0 m	35.0 m	40.0 m
200 m		76.2 cm	10	18.29 m	18.29 m	17.10 m
	FEMALE					
400 m	Adult	76.2 cm	10	45.0 m	35.0 m	40.0 m
200 m		76.2 cm	10	16.0 m	19.0 m	13.0 m

Table of Steeplechase specifications for a standard lap of 394 m.

Distance	Age Group	No. of Full Laps	No. of Hurdles	No. of Water Jumps	Distance Start to beginning 1st lap.	Distance of 1st hurdle after/ before beginning of 1st lap.
3000 m	Adult	7	28	7	242 m	-15.8 m
2000 m	U19	5	18	5	30 m	-203.8 m
1500 m	U17	3	13	3	318 m	+62.2 m
1000 m		2	8	2	212 m	-15.8 m

Hurdling

All hurdle races are sprint races and as such must be run in lanes. Specifications of barrier heights and spacing for different sexes and age groups are given in table 2.

Steeplechase

This event is restricted to males, and is basically a long distance hurdle, or obstacle, race. The lap is set out with four special hurdles, plus one water jump, which are successively negotiated according to the distance of the race.

The layout of a steeplechase course, for 1000m, 1500m, 2000m, and 3000m races is shown on page 8.

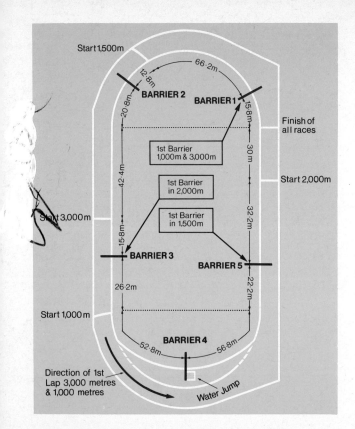

Start 1,500m

66·2m

12·8m

BARRIER 2

20·8m

BARRIER 1

15·8m

Finish of all races

30 m

1st Barrier 1,000m & 3,000m

42·4m

Start 2,000m

1st Barrier in 2,000m

32·2m

1st Barrier in 1,500m

15·8m

Start 3,000m

BARRIER 3

BARRIER 5

22·2m

26·2m

Start 1,000m

BARRIER 4

52·8m

56·8m

Direction of 1st Lap 3,000 metres & 1,000 metres

Water Jump

Layout of Steeplechase on a standard 400m track.

SPECIFICATIONS OF TRACK FURNITURE

Finishing Tape and Posts

A finishing tape *may* be stretched above the finish line at breast height, i.e. 1·22m above the ground, to *assist* the judges in placing the competitors. The tape should be of white 2-ply Botany wool, and not of man-made fibres since these can injure the athlete.

Posts supporting the finish tape should be placed at least 30cms from the edge of the track, and be at least 15cms higher than the tape, i.e. 1·37m.

Relay Baton

The baton is a smooth, hollow tube 28cms to 30cms long and 12cms in circumference. It must not weigh less than 50gms.

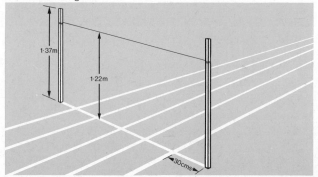

1·37m

1·22m

30cms

The Finish.

Hurdles

Whenever possible the International type of hurdle should be used. Other types of hurdles should conform to the overall dimensions of the International hurdle, and should be capable of being rigidly fastened at the required height.

The International hurdle should conform to the following specifications:

Overall width	120cms
Length of base	70cms
Depth of top bar	70mm
Thickness of top bar	10-25mm
Minimum total weight	10kgs

The toppling force required to overturn a hurdle should be between 3·6kgs and 4kgs and between 2·7kgs and 3kgs for athletes under 17 years.

The top bar should be striped in black and white, and where adjustable to different heights, should be capable of being rigidly fastened at each height.

Steeplechase

The hurdles are made of heavy timber so that they cannot be overturned easily. They should be 91·4cms high with a tolerance of 3mm above and below. Each should be at least 3·66m wide and have a top bar of 12·7cms thick.

At the water jump the hurdle must be firmly fixed. The water obstacle shall be 3·66m square in plan, and have an elevation which slopes from 70cms deep at the hurdle end to ground level at the farther end.

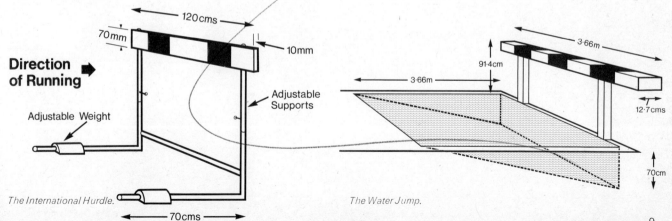

Direction of Running ➡

Adjustable Weight

Adjustable Supports

The International Hurdle.

The Water Jump.

9

COMPETITION RULES AND PROCEDURE

Competition is organised in limited classes according to the age of the competitor. The basic divisions are Under 15; Under 17; Under 19/20; and Adult, although females compete as adults from the age of 17. Unfortunately the age limits and the method of determining them differ slightly for the different governing bodies, i.e. the A.A.A., the W.A.A.A., the Scottish A.A.A. and the English Schools A.A. Accurate reference to minor detail on these matters, and on minor details of rule changes, is best made via the current rule book of the respective associations as the athlete or official becomes more deeply involved in the sport.

Pre Race

A draw for starting positions is made before the commencement of each race. It is usual for this to be made when the entries have been received, and as the programme is compiled, so that the lane draw can be published in the official programme of the meeting.

The Start

Optional use of starting blocks is permitted in scratch races up to and including 800m, and on the first leg of any relay (where this leg does not exceed 800 metres) but not in handicap races.

The athlete may use his own blocks with the approval of the starter. They must :

(a) be constructed of rigid materials;

(b) be without springs or similar devices;

(c) enable both feet to remain in contact with the ground during starting.

The blocks may be placed so that they protrude into an adjacent lane only provided that neither they, nor the athlete using them, obstruct and thereby endanger the safety of other competitors.

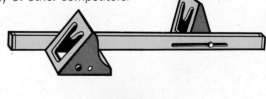

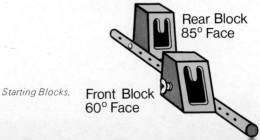

Rear Block
85° Face

Front Block
60° Face

Starting Blocks.

Sprints

Middle Distance

| ON YOUR MARKS | SET | GUN | ON YOUR MARKS | GUN |

At the beginning of the race the competitors will be placed by the marksman in their correct lanes and on the assembly line which is situated 3m behind the starting line.

At the command 'On your marks', the competitors should walk forward to the starting line and take up the appropriate position. At this and all subsequent stages competitors must remain behind the nearer edge of the starting line.

When all competitors are motionless the starter will command – 'Set!'

All competitors then assume their final 'Set' positions and again when all are motionless the *gun is fired.*

In races over 800m the command 'Set', is dispensed with, and replaced by 'On your marks'; then, when all are still, the gun is fired.

If competitors leave their mark with either hand or foot before the gun is fired, or if they take unnecessarily long in settling into position, they shall be considered to have committed a 'false start'. Any offender will first be warned, and after a subsequent infringement will be disqualified, except in the Decathlon and Pentathlon events where two false starts are permitted before disqualification.

False starts can be committed by more than one athlete at a time. When this occurs all offenders where identifiable shall be penalised.

11

During the Race

When running in lanes athletes *must* keep within the confines of their own lane. Those running outside their lane, or on the inner boundary line, risk disqualification; so do those who, during races not confined to lanes, run across, obstruct or jostle opponents so as to impede their progress.

The Finish

The order in which the athletes' torsos (excluding head, arms, hands, legs and feet) reach the nearer edge of the finish line determines the finishing order.

The Finish.

Relays

At the start of all relay races the baton must be held so that no part of it touches the ground beyond the starting line after the athlete has adopted the 'On your marks' position.

At each exchange the baton must change hands within the 20m take-over box. Failure to achieve this will result in the disqualification of the entire team.

Pushing, or assisting, during the exchange is not permitted. The baton must also be passed from hand to hand, and not thrown. If dropped, it must be retrieved by the person who dropped it.

During, and after, the exchange both runners must remain within their own lane until the course is clear. Athletes who wilfully impede members of opposing teams will themselves be disqualified, and thereby disqualify their team.

*Hand Holding
Baton correctly.*

Hurdling

Where International type hurdles are used competitors may knock over any number of barriers during a race without penalty. In instances where this type of hurdle is not used the maximum which may be knocked over without disqualification is TWO.

Hurdlers are not permitted to trail their foot or leg around the side of any barrier while clearing it. This rule creates problems for the 400m hurdler who leads naturally with his right leg, since during the race he is continually courting disaster when running around the bends.

Steeplechase

Competitors are permitted to jump, vault or place one foot on each barrier whilst negotiating it. At the water jump they are allowed to enter the water, without penalty, and good technique demands that the athlete steps onto the barrier with one foot, into the water at its shallower edge with the other, then out onto dry land at the next stride.

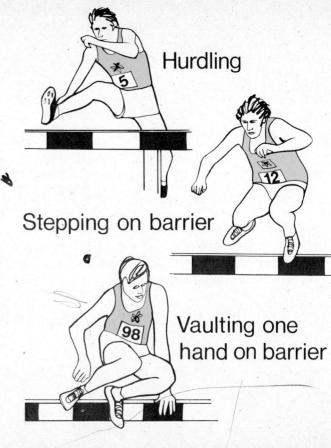

Hurdling

Stepping on barrier

Vaulting one hand on barrier

Jumping Rules

General

A draw is made before the competition, in the same manner as for track events, in order to decide the order of jumping. Competitors are not permitted to hold over trials to a later round, except in the vertical jumps (High Jump and Pole Vault).

The judges have the power to alter the order in special circumstances, e.g. when one or more competitors are entered in a track race and field event which take place at the same time, or when they are entered in two field events which take place at the same time. In such instances the change of order can only be made at the end of a round.

In special circumstances the judges are also empowered to change the site of a jumping competition, e.g. if the take-off area breaks up. This too may only be done at the end of a round.

Horizontal Jumps

In Long Jump and Triple Jump the competition is conducted in one of the following manners:

(a) by each competitor being given from three to six jumps;

(b) by each competitor having three jumps, and then the best three to eight competitors having a further three jumps;

(c) in championship meetings a qualifying distance may be selected and a qualifying competition of three trials held preceding the main competition.

Performances in the qualifying competition are ignored in determining final places.

Each jumper is credited with the best of his trials in the competition. In the case of a tie, the athlete achieving the better second best jump is awarded the higher placing. This procedure continues comparing third best jumps and so on if the tie cannot be resolved on the second best jump. If a tie still remains for first place the athletes jump again until it is resolved. For other places the tie remains.

The athlete is penalised if he:

(a) touches the ground between the take-off board and landing area (pit);

(b) walks back through the pit after landing;

(c) falls against the edge of the pit nearer the take-off board than where he landed;

(d) places check marks on the runway;

(e) uses handweights or grips of any sort.

Triple Jump

has the following additional rules:
- (*a*) The competitor is permitted to land between the take-off board and landing area without penalty provided that he:
  - (i) lands first on his take-off foot;
  - (ii) lands secondly on the opposite foot;
  - (iii) does not permit the inactive (sleeping) leg to touch the ground during any of the phases of the jump before the final landing.

Vertical Jumps

The competitor is permitted to commence jumping at any height above the minimum which he chooses, and to elect to jump at any subsequent height, until he records three successive failures, *irrespective of height*.

In instances where a tie occurs the premier place is awarded to the athlete who:
- (*a*) has least number of attempts at the height at which the tie occurs;
- (*b*) has the lowest total number of *failures* throughout the competition;
- (*c*) has the lowest total number of *jumps* throughout the competition.

Conditions (*b*) and (*c*) are only employed when the preceding condition fails to resolve the tie. If a tie still remains for first place the competitors *must* jump once more at that height, then the bar is raised or lowered (1cm in High Jump, 8cms in Pole Vault) at the discretion of the judges, until the tie is resolved. The athletes have no choice about jumping at this stage. Each height must be attempted.

Competitors are permitted to place marks, e.g. a handkerchief, on the bar to assist sighting.

A *failure* is recorded if the athlete:
- (*a*) dislodges the bar, either directly or indirectly;
- (*b*) touches the ground or landing area beyond the plane of the uprights without first clearing the bar.

|←——— **HOP** ———→|←——— **STEP** ———→|←——— **JUMP** ———→|

High Jump

The jumper may not take off simultaneously from both feet, neither may he use handweights to assist him.

The high jumper is the only athlete permitted to place checkmarks actually *on* the runway.

Pole Vault

The runway rules of the horizontal jumps apply to this event. The vaulter is permitted to:

(a) use his own pole without having to put it into the communal pool;

(b) bind the pole at the grip for a distance of 30cms with not more than two layers of adhesive tape to assist his hold;

(c) use adhesive rosin on his hands to further improve his grip on the pole, and to pad his forearm against injury from the pole;

(d) place sand in the planting 'box';

(e) adjust the uprights forwards or backwards up to a distance of 60cms from the back of the 'box'.

The vaulter may not:

(a) place his lower hand above the topmost one after take-off;

(b) leave the ground and fail to clear the bar without it being recorded as a failure.

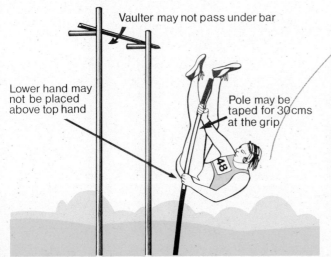

Vaulter may not pass under bar

Lower hand may not be placed above top hand

Pole may be taped for 30cms at the grip

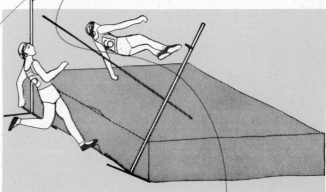

The jumper must not take off beyond the plane of the uprights nor dislodge the bar.

Jumps Specifications

Long Jump

The landing area should measure a minimum of 9m long by 2·75m wide. The sand in it should be moistened to assist accurate measuring, and be level with the surface of the take-off board.

The take-off board measures 1·22m long, by 20cms wide, and 10cms deep, and should be placed across the runway at least 1m from the nearer edge of the landing area (pit).

The runway should be between 40m and 45m long.

No-jump indication is facilitated by sprinkling the runway immediately on the pit side of the take-off board for a distance of 10cms from it with damp earth or sand. Alternatively this area can be covered with a plastic substance such as plasticine. Both sand or plasticine should be level with the surface of the take-off board.

Triple Jump

The landing area should measure 5·5m long by 2·75m wide. The sand should be moistened and level, just as for long jump.

The take-off board should be of the same dimensions as for long jump and should be placed across the runway at the following recommended distances depending upon the ability of the competitors:

(*a*) For Senior competitors — 11m.

(*b*) For Junior competitors — 9m or 10m.

At International level, however, the take-off board is at a safer distance if placed 12m to 13m from the pit. Similarly for jumpers of young ages (12 to 14 years old) distances of 7m to 8m are more suitable.

Lack of attention to detail in these matters can lead to quite serious injuries to competitors.

The runway should be between 40m and 45m long.

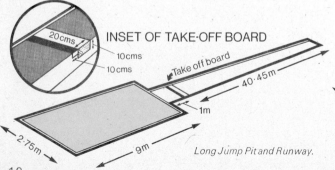

INSET OF TAKE-OFF BOARD

20cms
10cms
10cms

Take off board

40·45m

1m

2·75m

9m

Long Jump Pit and Runway.

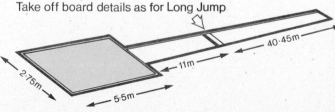

Take off board details as for Long Jump

40·45m

11m

2·75m

5·5m

Triple Jump Pit and Runway.

High Jump

The landing area should measure 5m by 4m. No stipulation is made as to the type of material which it should contain, although sand is most common. The filling should be soft enough to prevent injury, and where possible built up to above the level of the take-off area. In such instances the filling material is best retained by the construction of earth or sandbag retaining walls on the three sides farthest from the take-off area.

Modern biscuit-type foam landing areas are to be preferred to sand, but where used should be capable of preventing the jumper from bottoming. Reputable manufacturers will give specific guarantees in this respect for their products. Accept nothing less.

Loose foam, or bagged foam, is not recommended. Safety cannot be assured, and it is therefore potentially very dangerous.

Commercial foam landing areas cost very little more than the hitherto conventional sand pit to install, and are safer and more versatile in use.

The take-off area should be level, well watered and free from pitting.

The runway should permit an approach run of not less than 15m at any angle on the take-off side of the pit. An approach distance of 18m is advised however.

The uprights must be rigid and placed at least 3·66m. apart. The supporting pegs should have a flat upper surface 4cms wide, and should extend 6cms *in the direction of the opposite upright*.

The crossbar may be of triangular or circular section, of 30mm diameter, and should be between 3·64m and 4m long. Bars of circular section should have either square or flattened ends where they are supported by the pegs.

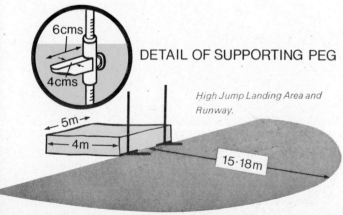

6cms

4cms

DETAIL OF SUPPORTING PEG

High Jump Landing Area and Runway.

5m

4m

15·18m

Pole Vault

The landing area should be 5m square in plan. No recommendation is made as to the material to be used, or the method of filling it, although the following are conventional:

(*a*) where sand is used, the surface of the pit should be built up at least 1m above the level of the take-off, in the manner described for High Jump;

(*b*) there should *not* be either a wooden or concrete retaining wall at the front, which can injure the vaulter;

(*c*) where commercial foam landing areas are used they should be constructed so that they prevent both bottoming, and rebounds from off the edges. These require a minimum depth of 60cms at club/school standard, and 90cms at International level.

The take-off is from a specially constructed box of the dimensions shown in the drawing. It is sunk into the runway so that its upper edge is level with the surface of the runway, and so that the back of the box is against the nearer edge of the landing area.

The runway should be between 40m and 45m long.

The uprights must be rigid and positioned at least 3·66m apart. They should be capable of being moved forward and backward up to 60cms from the back of the box with reasonable ease.

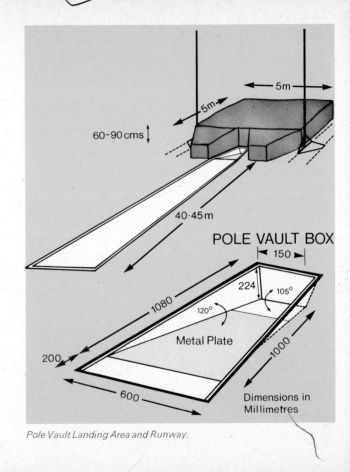

Pole Vault Landing Area and Runway.

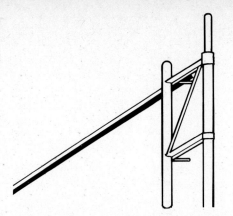

*Right Hand
Extension Arm.*

Supporting pegs for holding the cross-bar should be uniform and of 13mm diameter, and extend 7·5cms horizontally *in the direction of the landing area.* An extension arm may be attached to the uprights, thus permitting them to be placed further apart than the minimum distance and thereby increasing the safety of the vaulter.

The cross-bar should be of similar section as the high jump cross-bar, but between 3·86m and 4·52m long.

The vaulting pole may be constructed of any material, or combination of materials. The surface must be smooth.

Modern vaulting poles are of glass fibre construction and are designed specifically to perform under particular loadings, details of which are referred to in the Hints for the Competitor section of this booklet.

Throws Rules

General

A draw is made before the competition commences to decide the competition order, as for runs and jumps. Trials cannot be held over until later rounds except in special circumstances determined by the event judges.

Competitions are decided in a manner similar to that appertaining to the horizontal jumps, viz:

(a) by each competitor being given from three to six throws; or

(b) by each competitor having three throws, and then the best three to eight competitors having a further three throws;

(c) In championship meetings a qualifying distance may be selected and a qualifying competition of three trials held preceding the main competition. Performances in the qualifying competition cannot be carried over into the main competition.

Each competitor is credited with the best of his throws, ignoring performances set in qualifying competitions, and final placement, including resolution of ties, proceeds in parallel to that for horizontal jumps.

Competitors may not:

(a) place a target mark within the landing area (sector);

(b) wear protective gloves, except in the Hammer event;

(c) tape the hands or wrists for support unless in possession of a medical certificate confirming that the support is necessary to safeguard previous injuries;

(d) spread material on the surface of the circle in order to gain competitive advantage.

Competitors may:

(a) use their own implements provided that they are submitted to the referee for approval and, once approved, made available for the use of all competitors;

(b) use adhesive substances such as rosin on their hands in order to improve their grip.

When throwing from a circle the athlete must:

(a) commence from a stationary position;

(b) *not* touch either the top of the metal rim or stop-board, or the ground outside, after he has commenced to make his throw. He is permitted to touch the *inside* of the metal rim or stop-board without penalty;

(c) leave the circle *after* the implement has landed;

(d) retire from the *rear* half of the circle from a standing position.

The thrower may stop and restart his trial once without penalty. In the Hammer Throw there are special conditions under which this is permitted.

All implements must fall inside the inner edges of the sector lines in order to be valid.

FOUL   FOUL   FOUL

All Implements must fall inside inner edges of sector.

INVALID
INVALID
VALID

22

Shot Put

The shot must be *put* from the shoulder with one hand only. It must be kept in close proximity to the chin during the glide phase, and the hand must never be taken behind the line of the shoulders.

The shot putter is permitted to place his feet against the inside of the stop-board without penalty.

Hammer

The hammer thrower is permitted to wear a protective glove.

He is also permitted to stop a trial and recommence only provided that he does not stop as a result of the head of the hammer touching the ground or the surface of the circle. In such instances he is permitted to recommence provided that at no time is the hammer prevented from maintaining continuous motion.

Javelin

Although the javelin runway differs in construction from the other throwing platforms the basic principles of the rules do not differ from the other throws in that:

(a) the competitor is not permitted to step on the curved scratch line during, or after, the throw;

(b) at the moment of release he must be between the runway sidelines;

(c) he must remain within the confines of the runway, and behind the scratch line, until after the implement has landed;

(d) he must retire from behind the scratch line, or extensions of the scratch line.

In addition very specific rules control the manner in which the javelin is carried and thrown, viz:

(a) the javelin must be held at the grip, with one hand only;

(b) it must be held so that the little finger is nearest the point;

(c) the javelin must be thrown over the upper part of the shoulder or throwing arm;

(d) the javelin must not be slung or hurled;

(e) at no time after preparing to throw, and until after the javelin is released, is the thrower permitted to turn so that his back is towards the landing area.

As if these rules were not explicit enough the added statement that *'non-orthodox styles are not permitted'* is included in the rules.

A throw is invalidated if the *tip* of the metal head does not strike the ground before the remainder of the shaft when landing. *No rule exists which indicates that the javelin must stick in the ground or even that it must make a mark in order for the throw to be valid.*

The runway rules relating to the placement of check-marks which apply to the horizontal jumps also apply to Javelin.

Throws Specifications

Shot Put

Throwing Area

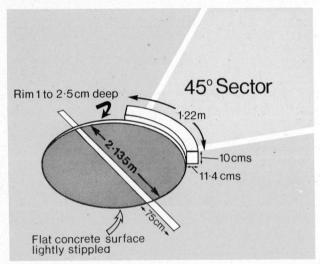

Rim 1 to 2·5 cm deep

45° Sector

1·22m

2·135m

10cms

11·4 cms

75cm

Flat concrete surface lightly stippled

The circle should be of 2·135m inside diameter, and may be indicated by a painted white line, 5cms wide, although it is preferable that an iron band measuring 7·5cms deep by 6mm thick be sunk into the ground so that its upper edge is at ground level.

The surface of the circle should be between 1cm and 2·5cms lower than the upper edge of the rim, and should be flat, and made of concrete. The surface should be trowelled so that the sand comes through to the surface of the mix, and produces a finished texture like sandpaper. Heavily stippled surfaces are not advised.

The landing area (sector) should be marked by extended radii, at the front of the circle, enclosing a sector of 45° between their inner edges.

A curved wooden stop-board should be fixed so that its inner edge coincides with that of the rim, and so that it spans the intersection of the radii and the circle rim equally. It should measure 1·22m long, by 11·4cms wide, by 10cms high.

Implements

The shot is constructed of either solid metal which is not softer than brass, or a shell of similar substance filled to the correct weight with another metal.

The following weight specifications apply to competition implements in the age groups listed:

Table of Shot weight specifications:—

	Under 15	15-17	17-19	Adult
Male	4 kg	5 kg	6.25 kg	7.257 kg
Female	3.25 kg	4 kg	4 kg	4 kg

Discus

Throwing Area

The circle has an inside diameter of 2·5m. No stop-board is used.

Otherwise specifications are identical with those for shot put, including a 45° landing sector.

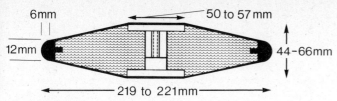

6mm

12mm

50 to 57 mm

44–66mm

219 to 221mm

Implements

The discus shall be composed of a smooth metal rim, attached to a body of wood or other suitable material (metal or plastic) and conform to the dimensions shown in the drawing. Junior implements are proportionately smaller.

The following weight specifications apply:

Table of Discus weight specifications:—

	Under 15	15-17	17-19	Adult
Male	1.25 kg	1.5 kg	1.75 kg	2 kg
Female	1 kg	1 kg	1 kg	1 kg

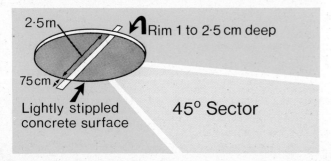

2·5 m

Rim 1 to 2·5 cm deep

75 cm

Lightly stippled concrete surface

45° Sector

Hammer
Throwing Area

The Hammer circle and throwing sector are identical in specification to that for shot put, except that no stop-board is used, and that the final finish of the circle should be slightly smoother than for discus or shot.

Implements

The head of the hammer should be constructed to the same specifications as for shot put, except that minimum diameters are slightly less in order to include the attachment of wire and handle, and still achieve the same overall weight.

The wire shall be a single length of spring steel wire of No. 11 Standard Wire Gauge, looped at both ends for attachment.

The handle must be incapable of stretching, and have no hinged joints.

Connections are by means of a loop at the handle, and either a plain, or ball-bearing swivel, plus loop, at the head.

The overall permitted length of the hammer is between 117·5cms and 121·5cms, measured under reasonable tension.

The following weight specifications apply:

Table of Hammer weight specifications:—

	Under 15	15-17	17-19	Adult
Male	4 kg	5 kg	6.25 kg	7.257 kg

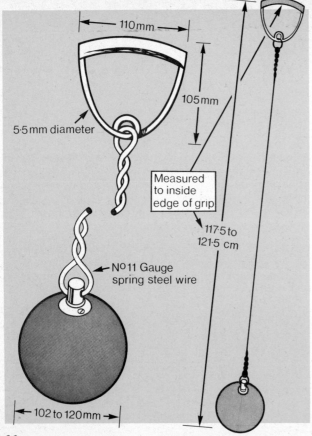

110mm

105mm

5·5mm diameter

Measured
to inside
edge of grip

117·5 to
121·5 cm

N°11 Gauge
spring steel wire

102 to 120mm

Javelin

Throwing Area

The runway shall be between 30m and 36·5m long and marked by two parallels, 5cms wide and 4m apart.

The scratch line shall be the arc of a circle of 8m radius drawn across the end of the runway nearer the landing area, and should be **7cms** wide.

Where it intersects the parallels of the runway, the scratch line should be extended at right angles to them for a distance of 1·5m.

Where constructed in wood or metal the scratch line should be sunk flush with the ground.

The landing area is enclosed by radii of the circle of which the scratch line is an arc, extended through the points at which it intersects the runway parallels. This will enclose a landing area of approximately 29°.

Implements

The javelin shall consist of a shaft, a cord grip, and a metal head, and must conform to the measurements shown in the drawing. Junior implements have proportionately reduced dimensions.

The cord must be placed about the centre of gravity of the javelin, under which should be the point of maximum circumference. The taper from this point to the tip, and rear, must be uniform.

The centre of gravity must be between 90cms and 110cms from the metal tip.

The cross section of the implement must be circular.

Table of Javelin weight specifications:—

	Under 15	15-17	17-19	Adult
Male	600 gms	700 gms	800 gms	800 gms
Female	600 gms	600 gms	600 gms	600 gms

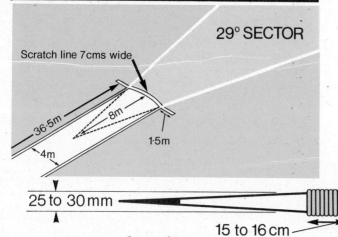

29° SECTOR

Scratch line 7cms wide

36·5m

8m

1·5m

4m

25 to 30 mm

25 to 33 cms

15 to 16 cm

90 to 110 cms

260 to 270 cms

Cord shall not exceed overall circumference by more than 25 mm

Cord grip must be about the Centre of Gravity

OFFICIATING

Runs

Judging

1. Be prepared to produce written results even in wet weather.
2. Carry your own notepad, and clipboard.
3. Stand well back from the finish, raised up if possible, with both finish posts in line.
4. Concentrate on the finish and not on the race as it progresses.
5. Try to determine the first *three* runners, and more if possible.
6. In deciding race positions parts of the body other than the *torso* must be discounted.
7. Write down the order immediately, before memory fades.

Timekeeping

1. See that your stopwatch is kept well maintained, and accurate.
2. Always operate the watch in a constant manner.
3. Where necessary, take up the 'first pressure' on the button before depressing it.
4. Once the athletes are 'Under starters orders', concentrate on the gun to the exclusion of everything else.
5. Start the watch on the flash, or smoke, which is visible before the report is heard.
6. Time runners, *not* places.
7. Concentrate on the finish posts until the *torso* of the incoming runner breaks the line of vision.
8. At this instant stop the watch.
9. Avoid anticipating the finish. Try to obtain a uniform reaction at both start and finish.
10. In timing places other than first, watch your runner to within 10m of the finish, then transfer your attention to the finish line.

Field Events

General

1. Be prepared to work in the wettest weather, and be capable of writing results in these conditions.
2. It pays to be self-sufficient. Therefore carry your own:

Clipboard   Measuring tape
Drawcards   Measuring spike
Marking pegs

3. Always act fairly and in the best interests of the competitors.

Before the event check the competition area and make good any deficiencies where possible.

In Vertical Jumps:

(*a*) mark the upper side of the cross-bar clearly;
(*b*) check that the landing area is safe;
(*c*) check that the uprights function correctly;
(*d*) check that roller, spade and rake are available.

In Horizontal Jumps:

(*a*) check that the sand is soft, moist and level;
(*b*) check that the provisions for indicating no-jumps are adequate, and that they can be maintained in good order throughout the competition;
(*c*) check that roller, rake and trowel are available.

In Throws:

1. check that safety measures are adequate;
2. check the throwing surface, and brush clean if necessary;
3. check implements;
4. check measuring equipment, tape, marking pegs and measuring spike;
5. see that a brush is available plus audible warning apparatus for sector judges;
6. check in the competitors, make the competition draw, and notify the athletes;
7. supervise the warm-up and see that it is conducted in a safe manner.

	COMPETITION	HIGH JUMP POLE VAULT	1ST TRIAL	2ND TRIAL	3RD TRIAL	BEST	PLACE	4TH TRIAL	5TH TRIAL	6TH TRIAL	FINAL BEST	FINAL PLACE
	VENUE	LONG JUMP TRIPLE JUMP DISCUS, JAVELIN, WEIGHT, HAMMER										
DATE	EVENT											
N°.	NAME	CLUB/COUNTRY										

RESULT	FT.	INS.	METRES	STANDARDS
1st				
2nd				
3rd				REFEREE / JUDGE
4th				JUDGE / JUDGE
5th				OBTAINABLE FROM
6th				**AMATEUR ATHLETIC ASSOCIATION**

Field Events Scorecard.

During the competition measure each trial, especially in throws, immediately after it is made. Efficiently carried out, this method is just as quick as that of pegging each throw, and then measuring at the end of the competition. It avoids the possibility of implements knocking other competitors' pegs out of the ground.

When measuring, place the *zero* end of the tape at the mark, and the *running* end through the scratch line or take-off board, where the distance is read off at the side farthest from the mark.

The distance of all jumps and shot put is measured to the nearest 1cm below the distance shown on the tape. The longer throws (discus, hammer, and javelin) are measured to the nearest *even* centimetre below the distance on the tape.

At the vertical jumps measure the distance between the ground and the uppermost part of the cross-bar at its lowest point, with a steel tape, each time that the bar is raised to a new height, or immediately after a record has been made.

Each time that the bar has been dislodged, ensure that it is replaced so that its uppermost edge is the same as before it was dislodged.

Keep the take-off in good repair.

At the throwing area listen for the implement landing while continuing to watch for foot infringements. Don't forget to check the exit from the circle.

In shot put, stand at the side of the circle to watch for hand infringements.

Replace so that mark indicating upper side is correct

Measure to upper side of bar

At the throws landing area try to anticipate where the implement will land by taking trouble to familiarise yourself with the capabilities of the competitors before the competition begins.

Take care to watch the implement onto the ground. If it fails to make a mark, you must be able to pinpoint accurately its point of landing.

Beware of implements in flight and take early evasive action if necessary.

When measuring place the zero end of the tape on that part of the mark made by the implement which is nearest to the scratch line. Ignore marks made by the tail of the javelin, or the handle of the hammer.

Place tape on mark nearest to the scratch line

COMPETING

Clothing

Initially you will require little equipment. Specialised clothing is not absolutely necessary at first. A vest, shorts or knickers, plus plimsolls will suffice. Running shoes, or spikes as they are called, are a desirable alternative to plimsolls, but are not essential.

For outdoor work in cold weather warm overclothing such as a tracksuit is advisable, but here again an old jumper and trousers will provide a cheap and functional alternative. Additional optional extras may include a long sleeved football jersey, a woollen hat and gloves, and tights for use in the very coldest conditions.

As you become more proficient the need for specialist equipment, particularly footwear, will increase. The better quality running spikes have a padded heel to prevent injury. Special jumping spikes include this together with a six-spike sole. The high jump shoe has a sole which is built up to a thickness of 13mm, and has spikes in the heel. Throwing shoes are flat soled, and hammer shoes have a special sole construction of curved section. Javelin boots are high sided for support, and have six long spikes, two of which are placed in the heel. Because they are specially made for a limited market these shoes are more costly than standard products.

Special hammer gloves can be obtained through good sports shops, although during the early stages of learning the event an old leather glove will serve quite adequately. Plastic heel cups for jumpers, especially triple jumpers, may be obtained through the Kangaroo Club.

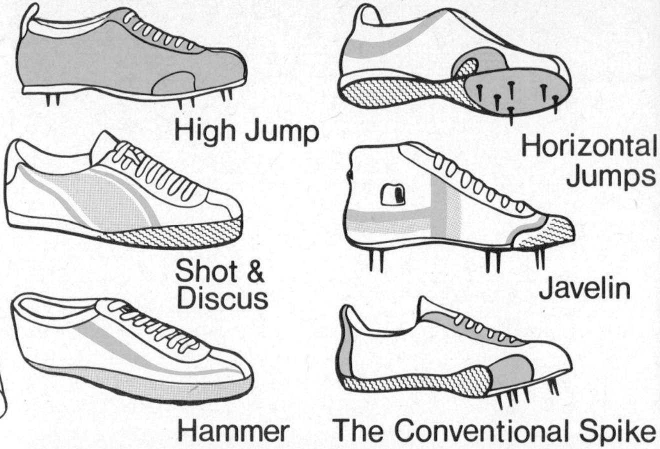

High Jump

Horizontal Jumps

Shot & Discus

Javelin

Hammer

The Conventional Spike

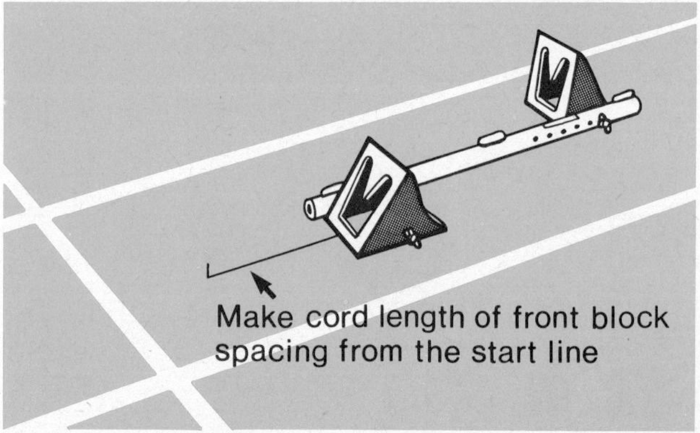

Make cord length of front block spacing from the start line

Competition

General

Wear the correct numbers front and back in races up to and including 400m. In races over this distance, and in field events, organisers may provide only one number. This is worn on the breast. Numbers must always be visible.

Warm up in good time for your competition, at least half an hour before it starts, and be on hand when required by the officials.

In track events

Keep warm, in your tracksuit, until under starter's orders.

Remember that you are not permitted help in placing your starting blocks. A piece of cord of the correct length attached to the front of the block will help you to measure the distance from the starting line both quickly and accurately.

Don't forget your starting block fixing pins, and a hammer.

Always carry spare spikes of varying lengths, together with a spike spanner and spare laces.

Safety pins with which to attach numbers are a necessity.

In field events it is good manners to remove your tracksuit while the preceding competitor is completing his trial, so that you are ready to enter the throwing area or runway as soon as the officials call you.

Jumps

Always measure run-ups in 'foot-lengths' and not with a measuring tape. Your feet cannot be left at home.

After your warm up arrive at the event in sufficient time to measure, and make any necessary adjustments to, your approach run.

Try to be prepared for inclement weather by having waterproofs and/or a change of clothing with you.

Check your take-off position after each jump, and make adjustments if necessary.

In vertical jumps decide beforehand those heights which you are going to attempt, and inform the judge of your intentions at the beginning of each round.

Avoid unnecessary jumps at low heights.

Try to organise the number of attempts that you make so that peak performance coincides with the greater heights.

Keep warm and supple between trials.

Vaulters should always remember to carry a tin of rosin, and a roll of adhesive tape.

Choose your glass-fibre pole carefully. They are labelled according to the optimum loadings which will bend them, when held at a specific height. Thus a 140–14 will perform best at 140lb loadings held at 14ft. Roughly speaking it is the correct pole for a vaulter of 140lbs weight, although one must remember that loadings include the force generated by the athlete's approach run and therefore the 140lb vaulter will most probably require either a 150 or 160 pole depending upon his strength and ability. The higher the vaulter moves his grip the floppier the pole will become and vice-versa. Fibre-glass vaulters must therefore progress from one pole to another as they develop their ability.

Thank the judges at the end of the competition.

Throwers

Warm up at least 30 minutes before the competition is due to start, and include much suppling of the joint complexes directly involved.

Keep practice throws to a minimum in order to keep adrenalin locked away ready to be released on the first throw. Mental rehearsal and assistance drills are better than throwing at this stage.

Obey the safety instructions of the judges, both before and during the competition.

Don't be afraid to brush loose material from off the circle before your trial if necessary.

Be ready to throw when called for by the judge.

You will need a dry cloth with which to dry wet implements during bad weather, plus rosin for Discus or Javelin in order to improve grip.

Thank the judges after the event.

RIGHT

keep warm & supple between jumps, if necessary under a blanket

WRONG

RIGHT

DECATHLON AND PENTATHLON

These are the 'Blue Riband' events of athletics, and as such are competitions for the best all-rounders.

The decathlon is for men and takes place over two days, and includes ten events which are held in the following order:

First Day – 100m; Long Jump; Shot Put; High Jump; and 400m.

Second Day – 110m Hurdles; Discus; Pole Vault; Javelin; and 1500m.

The Pentathlon is mainly for women, although young men compete in the event as a build-up to the greater demands of the Decathlon. It comprises five events held in the following order:

Women – 100m Hurdles; Shot Put; High Jump; Long Jump; 200m.

Men – Long Jump; Javelin; 200m; Discus; 1500m.

In a Junior Pentathlon the choice of events and implements is at the discretion of the organisers.

It is possible, at the discretion of the promoters, to hold the Decathlon on *one* day, in which case it is also permitted to change the order of events. Promoters are similarly empowered to hold the women's Pentathlon over two days, if they wish.

The Competition

Points are awarded to each competitor for his best performance in each individual event according to a scale compiled by the International Amateur Athletic Federation and published by them in booklet form.

The competitor achieving the highest grand total over the competition as a whole is the winner.

In the event of a tie the higher place is awarded to the competitor who has placed higher in a majority of events, or if a tie still remains to the one who has recorded the highest single score throughout the competition.

Three trials only are permitted in Long Jump, Shot Put, Discus, and Javelin. In order to balance this ruling *two* false starts are permitted in track events before disqualification.

In races, excluding the 1500m, competitors run in groups of three or four individuals.

The 1500m event should be seeded so that the leading five or six competitors at the end of the nine preceding events compete directly against each other for the premier places.

Failure to take part in an event brings about automatic exclusion from the remainder of the competition. This does *not* apply in instances where athletes compete in events but fail to register a score, e.g. when they record three no-throws in a throwing event.

When timekeeping at least two watches are required to record the time of each competitor. In instances where only two watches are used, and the times differ, the slower time must be the one awarded to the competitor.

	Running events			Hurdles	Jumping events			Throwing events		
	100 m	400 m	1.500 m	110 m	🏃	🏃	🏃	●	◉	
	sec.	sec. min.	min.	sec.	cm	cm	cm	m	m	m
350	-	-	5.11,1	21,8	-	491	-	8,56	24,79	31,15
349	-	1.02,8	5.11,3	-	-	-	243	8,54	24,75	31,09
348	-	-	5.11,5	-	-	-	-	8,53	24,71	31,03
347	-	-	5.11,7	-	-	490	-	8,52	24,67	30,98
346	-	1.02,9	5.11,9	-	-	-	-	8,50	24,63	30,92
345	-	-	5.12,1	21,9	-	-	-	8,49	24,59	30,86
344	-	-	5.12,3	-	145	489	242	8,48	24,55	30,80
343	-	1.03,0	5.12,5	-	-	-	-	8,47	24,51	30,74
342	-	-	5.12,7	-	-	488	241	8,45	24,47	30,69
341	-	-	5.12,9	-	-	-	-	8,44	24,43	30,63
340	-	1.03,1	5.13,1	22,0	-	487	-	8,43	24,39	30,57
								8,42	24,35	30,51
339	13,3	-	5.13,5	-	-	-	240	8,40	24,31	30,45
								8,39	24,27	30,40

Extract from Men's Decathlon Table.

PENTATHLON - 200 metres - (1/100 sec) - 200 mètres

Secs.	Points	Secs.	Points	Secs.	Points	Secs.	Points	Secs.	Points
24,10	928	24,60	882	25,10	838	25,60	795	26,10	754
11	927	61	881	11	837	61	794	11	753
12	926	62	880	12	836	62	793	12	753
13	925	63	879	13	835	63	793	13	752
14	924	64	878	14	834	64	792	14	751
15	923	65	877	15	833	65	791	15	750
16	922	66	877	16	832	66	790	16	749
17	922	67	876	17	832	67	789	17	749
18	921	68	875	18	831	68	788	18	748
19	920	69	874	19	830	69	788	19	747
24,20	919	24,70	873	25,20	829	25,70	787	26,20	746
21	918	71	872	21	828	71	786	21	745
22	917	72	871	22	827	72	785	22	745
23	916	73	870	23	826	73	784	23	744
				24	826	74	783	24	743

Extract from Women's Pentathlon Table, reproduced with the permission of the I.A.A.F.

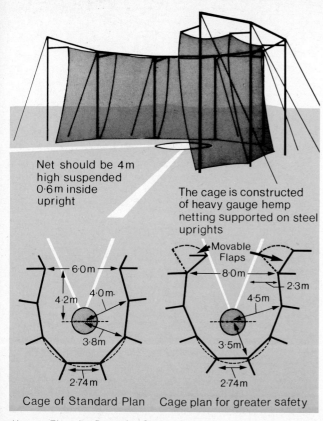

Net should be 4m high suspended 0·6m inside upright

The cage is constructed of heavy gauge hemp netting supported on steel uprights

6·0m

4·0m

4·2m

3·8m

2·74m

Cage of Standard Plan

Movable Flaps

8·0m

2·3m

4·5m

3·5m

2·74m

Cage plan for greater safety

Hammer Throwing Protection Cage.

SAFETY

Safety considerations affecting athletics are complex in their range and magnitude. Most of us are aware that precautions need to be taken to ensure the safety of competitors, officials and spectators when events such as Javelin and Hammer are in progress. Less obvious problems arise concerning the safe organisation of training and practice for these and other events. Prevention of injury resulting from poor maintenance of the track and its furniture, and from bad training habits are other important safety aspects which will be discussed in this chapter.

Throws

1. **Competition.** For Discus and Hammer, use of a safety cage conforming to the pattern approved by the I.A.A.F. is advised.

The landing area should be further roped off at a height of 1m above ground level enclosing a sector of *60°*. The Javelin and Shot Put landing areas should be similarly enclosed at a distance of 2m outside the sector lines.

A restraining net should enclose the Discus and Javelin landing areas, being attached to the stakes supporting the rope barrier, in order to arrest the implement on landing.

During practice before the competition all throwing should occur only from the competition circle or runway. Judges are responsible for supervision, and are empowered to disqualify athletes who after warning are wilfully unco-operative.

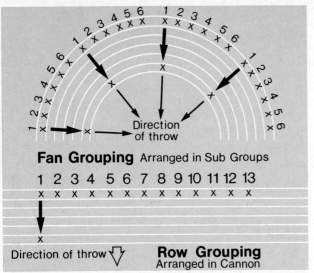

Fan Grouping Arranged in Sub Groups

1 2 3 4 5 6 7 8 9 10 11 12 13

x x x x x x x x x x x x x

x

Direction of throw ⬇ **Row Grouping**
Arranged in Cannon

2. **Training.** Generally speaking the restrictions which govern competition apply in the training situation. In group training or teaching situations the following further precautions are advised:

(*a*) the 'whole-group' approach is safer and better than the 'small sub-groups' approach. Young athletes *must not* be permitted to throw unsupervised;

(*b*) when organising groups:
  (i) time can be saved by adopting the 'all throw – all retrieve' principle;
  (ii) organisation of the group in 'fan' or 'rows' permits all to throw simultaneously;
  (iii) in this situation adequate spacing of athletes is important;
  (iv) arrangement of the group in numbered sub-groups increases the safety spacing between throwers. Thus ones step forward and throw, then twos, and so on. When all have thrown – all retrieve;
  (v) throwing 'in cannon' permits quick individual supervision within the 'whole group' situation.

(*c*) walk when carrying implements, especially javelins;

(*d*) javelins should be carried vertically, point down;

(*e*) when removing javelins from the ground push them upright then pull them out vertically;

(*f*) never stand behind a person with a javelin;

(*g*) never stand on the high point side of a Hammer Thrower or the throwing arm side of a Discus Thrower;

(*h*) never throw towards anyone;

(*i*) never walk in front of a thrower;

(*j*) never throw from wet grass;

3. **Maintenance** Nylon safety nets, whilst being resistant to water, will rot from exposure to sunlight. Therefore check them frequently, and replace when necessary.

Frequently check discoi for loosening of the locking screw and tighten it if necessary.

Dry discoi after use in wet weather.

Store javelins vertically.

Hang hammers from a hook so that the wire is fully extended. Keep the spindles free of soil, and well oiled. Chain hammers reduce the risk of damage to the playing surface, and that of potential damage to an unfortunate recipient in case of an accident.

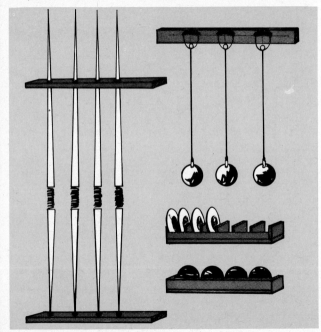

Storage of Throwing Implements.

Jumps

1. Competition. The nature of the jumping events does not make them dangerous in themselves, with the possible exception of Pole Vault.

The roping off of the landing area and runway will prevent unauthorised persons from endangering competitors by wandering across the runway.

Landing areas should be constructed to specification, particularly in the vertical jumps.

2. Maintenance. Landing areas should be kept full of sand, and well dug. They should also be kept free from buried broken glass.

Vertical jump landing areas should be checked yearly for signs of deterioration of the foam, and replaced if necessary.

Take-off boards should always be flush with the surface of the runway.

Runways should be raked, levelled, and watered regularly.

Where dual purpose Long Jump/Triple Jump provision is made, the Long Jump take-off board should not be sited so that it corresponds with the landing position of the Triple Jump step phase.

3. Athletes. Wear heel cups to prevent bruising of the heel.

Badly worn spikes can cause foot injuries, particularly to triple jumpers.

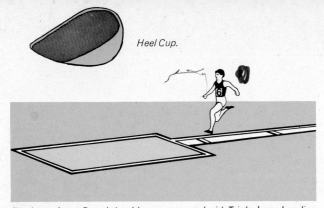

Heel Cup.

The Long Jump Board should not correspond with Triple Jump Landing.

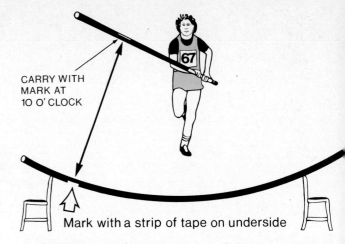

CARRY WITH
MARK AT
10 O'CLOCK

Mark with a strip of tape on underside

Vaulters should take good care of glass-fibre poles. Store them off the ground. Never use them cold or slightly damaged. Always ensure that the direction of the bend is clearly marked. This can be found by balancing the pole on two chairs and letting it sag in the middle. Mark the sag clearly with tape, and in use keep this at 10 o'clock.

Runs

1. **Maintenance.** It is important that furniture such as hurdles and steeplechase barriers are kept in good repair. Hurdles should be painted and greased each winter.

The floor of the steeplechase waterjump should be secure, and barrier tops should be replaced when they become so worn as to be dangerous to the athletes using them.

2. **Athletes.** Careful maintenance of clothing and shoes will prevent minor irritations and injuries.

More serious injury can result from injudicious training habits. Too severe training involving sudden increases of training loads, excessive racing, lack of sleep, and training on hard surfaces can lead to loss of weight, swollen glands, rashes, backache and loss of form. More serious conditions such as strains, torn muscles, inflammation of tendons, and even stress fractures of the lower leg can occur.

Such illness and injury can be prevented by safe conduct of training programmes so that the situations which cause them are avoided. Prevention is always better than cure!

40